Helping Children See Jesus

ISBN: 978-1-64104-036-5

Prophets of Messiah
Old Testament Volume 32: Isaiah, Jeremiah, Lamentations, Ezekiel, Daniel

Authors: Ruth B. Greiner, Katherine E. Hershey,
Arlene S. Piepgrass and others
Illustrator: Vernon Henkel
Colorization: Olivia and Bethany Moy
Typesetting and Layout: Patricia Pope

© 2019 Bible Visuals International
PO Box 153, Akron, PA 17501-0153
Phone: (717) 859-1131
www.biblevisuals.org

All rights reserved. No part of this publication may be reproduced, stored in a retrieval system or transmitted in any form by any means, electronic, mechanical, photocopy, recording or otherwise, without the prior permission of the publisher, except as provided by USA copyright law.

RELATED ITEMS

To access related items (such as activities, memory verse posters and translated texts) please visit our web store at www.biblevisuals.org and enter 2032 at the top right of the web page. You may need to reduce the zoom setting to get the search box.

FREE TEXT DOWNLOAD

To obtain a FREE printable copy of the English teaching text (PDF format) under Product Format, please scroll down and select Extra–PDF Teacher Text Download. Then under Language select English before clicking the ADD TO CART button to place in your shopping cart. Other languages are available at an additional cost from the Language menu. When checking out, use coupon code XTACSV17 at checkout and click on Apply Coupon to receive the discount on the English text.

All we like sheep have gone astray; we have turned every one to his own way; and the LORD hath laid on Him the iniquity of us all. Isaiah 53:6

Obey My voice, and I will be your God, and ye shall be My people: and walk ye in all the ways I have commanded you, that it may be well unto you. Jeremiah 7:23

"And I will make them one nation in the land . . . and one King shall be King to them all . . . I will cleanse them . . . and I will be their God."

Ezekiel 37:22, 23

"The Most High ruleth in the kingdom of men, and giveth it to whomsoever He will."

Daniel 4:32b

MESSIAH = CHRIST

Old Testament   **New Testament**
Hebrew word   **Greek word**

meaning

THE ANOINTED ONE

Lesson 1
ISAIAH: THE MESSIAH PROVIDES SALVATION

NOTE TO THE TEACHER

For your study of these Major Prophets, we recommend the book *The Prophets Still Speak (Messiah In Both Testaments)* by Fred John Meldau. If your Christian bookstore does not have it, order directly from the publisher: Friends of Israel, Bellmawr, NJ, 08099.

Occasionally in this series we have recommended that you obtain a *Ryrie Study Bible*. Because it is a *study* Bible, the notes throughout every book of the Bible are invaluable. It is presently available in the *King James Version, The New King James Version, New American Standard Version*, and the *New International Version (NIV)*. The *NIV* includes some additional pages of excellent teaching material. If this Bible is not available in your Christian book store, order from the publisher: Moody Press, Chicago, IL, 60610.

All the Old Testament prophets warned God's people of punishment if they turned away from Him. The Israelites (the Northern Kingdom) ignored the warnings and worshiped man-made idols. So God allowed them to be captured by the cruel Assyrians. Oh, how the Israelites suffered for their sins! (*Teacher:* See in this series Old Testament Volume 25, lesson 4.)

The people of Judah (the Southern Kingdom) knew the awfulness of idol-worship. They remembered how severely the Israelites had been punished. They heard the warnings of the prophets, *Isaiah* and *Jeremiah*. But they, too, turned away from God. So, like the Israelites, the people of Judah were forced from their homeland. And for 70 years they were captives in far-away Babylon. (See Old Testament Volume 26, lessons 1, 2 and 4.)

The people of Judah turned from God. But He never turned from them. Indeed, He sent with them to Babylon His prophets, *Ezekiel* and *Daniel*, to speak for Him. From *Daniel* they learned of *Messiah—The Anointed One* who would come from God.

The title of this volume introduces the name Messiah. It is used only a few times in the English King James version of the Bible. (See *Daniel* 9:25-26; John 1:41; 4:25-26.) *Messiah* (or *Messias*) is the Hebrew word for the Greek word *Christ*. Both *Messiah* and *Christ* mean *The Anointed One*—One set apart by God for Himself. Anointing was well-known in Bible times. Prophets, priests and kings were anointed with holy oil. They were thus set apart for the work of God. (See 1 Kings 19:16b; Exodus 29:5-7; 1 Samuel 16:1, 12-13.)

So *Messiah, Christ, The Anointed One*, would be a Prophet. (See Deuteronomy 18:15-19; compare John 6:14.) Also He would be a Priest. (See *Zechariah* 6:12-13; compare Hebrews 4:14-15.) And He would be the King. (See *Isaiah* 9:6-7; compare Luke 1:31-33; Acts 2:29-30; Revelation 15:3.) The anointing of Christ the *Messiah* was not with ordinary oil, however. He was anointed by the Holy Spirit of God. (See Matthew 3:16-17; Mark 9:2-7; Luke 4:17-18; John 1:32-34.)

Through *Isaiah, Jeremiah, Ezekiel* and *Daniel*, God revealed amazing prophecies. Many of these have already come true. Others are even yet to be fulfilled. For this study, only a few chapters are used from each of these prophetic books. For example, the focus in lesson #1 is on the One who would come to save sinners. Although He is not named, we know from the New Testament that Isaiah prophesied of Christ.

Because many truths are included in this lesson, some of the illustration pages have multiple sketches. If these would confuse your students, cover all but the first illustration. (A tiny drop of paste or a paper clip would keep each cover in place.) Remove covers as you come to succeeding illustrations.

Each lesson in this volume may be divided into two, three or four lessons. The prophets' names are printed in bold type to help you spot them and their prophecies.

Display often the outside back cover so your students will remember:

MESSIAH = CHRIST
Old Testament   New Testament
Hebrew word   Greek word
meaning: THE ANOINTED ONE

Scripture to be studied: Isaiah chapters 1, 6-7, 9, 52-53

The *aim* of the lesson: To show that ages ago through Isaiah the prophet, God revealed that Christ the Savior would come to earth.

What your students should *know*: God, the holy One, cannot tolerate sin.

What your students should *feel*: Hatred for their own sin.

What your students should *do*: Believe that Christ died for their sins and receive Him as their Savior.

Lesson outline (for the teacher's and students' notebooks):
1. God's call to sinners (Isaiah 1:1-31).
2. God's commission to service (Isaiah 6:1-13).
3. God's promise of a Savior (Isaiah 7:1-15; 9:6-7).
4. God's provision of salvation (Isaiah 52:1-53:12).

The verse to be memorized:

All we like sheep have gone astray; we have turned every one to his own way; and the LORD hath laid on Him the iniquity of us all. (Isaiah 53:6)

THE LESSON

In the beginning of time, Satan caused Eve and Adam to sin. Immediately God promised to send to earth Someone who would finally crush Satan. (See Genesis 3:15; Revelation 20:10.) We know from the New Testament something which Adam and Eve could not know: the One whom God would send is the Lord Jesus Christ. God repeated this promise many, many times. The writers of the Old Testament used several names for Him. Often they simply spoke of Him as "He." But in the New Testament we learn who "He" is.

Today we begin a study of four (4) very interesting prophets: **Isaiah**, **Jeremiah**, **Ezekiel**, and **Daniel**. Each of these prophets told about the One who would come. Each prophet used various names when speaking of Him. Because **Daniel** used the name *Messiah* (**Daniel** 9:25-26), these lessons are titled *PROPHETS OF MESSIAH*. (*Teacher:* Show outside front cover.)

Daniel spoke the Hebrew language of the Old Testament. In Hebrew, *Messiah* means *The Anointed One*—One set apart by God for Himself. In Greek, the language of the New Testament, *Christ* also means *The Anointed, set apart, One*. (*Teacher:* Display outside back cover.) So *Messiah*, the One promised in the Old Testament, is *Christ* who came in New Testament times. He is the Anointed One, set apart by God for His purpose.

The prophet **Isaiah** told more about *Messiah/Christ* than any other Old Testament writer. Yet he never mentions either name! Listen carefully!

1. GOD'S CALL TO SINNERS
Isaiah 1:1-31

God was very sad. He loved the people of Judah, but they had turned against Him. For this reason, He would have to punish them. Before doing so, He would urge them to return to Him. So this is what God did: to **Isaiah**, one of His prophets, God gave a vision. It was like a big picture in the sky.

Show Illustration #1

Isaiah looked up and saw God (point to #1B) the Judge of all the earth, sitting on His throne. **Isaiah** heard God say to His people, "I have chosen you to be My children. I gave you the land where you live. I have protected you from your enemies. But you have rebelled against Me. You are a sinful nation, loaded with guilt. You have turned away (point to #1C) from Me, the Holy One." (See **Isaiah** 1:2-6.)

The Lord God continued, "I am not pleased with the sacrifices you offer to Me. You say you love Me. But your hearts are turned from Me. Even if you say many prayers, I shall not listen." (See **Isaiah** 1:11-15.) Then God begged His people, saying: "Stop doing wrong. Learn to do right."

Because of His love, God reached out saying, "Come to Me. Even though your sins are like scarlet, they shall be as white as snow. Though they are red as crimson, they shall be like wool." (Point to #1D.) Then God promised, "If you will listen and obey Me, I shall forgive you." (See **Isaiah** 1:18-19.)

The scarlet and red colors in Bible times were too bright to be washed out. But God was willing to forgive even the worst sins of His people. And He would do so if they returned to Him, asking His forgiveness. Just so, He is willing to forgive your sins today.

2. GOD'S COMMISSION TO SERVICE
Isaiah 6:1-13

Later, **Isaiah** had another vision of the Lord. (*Teacher:* If your students have Bibles, let them follow verses covering this part of the lesson.)

Show Illustration #2

Isaiah saw the Lord sitting on a high throne in the temple. (See **Isaiah** 6:1-3.) Above the throne were angel-like beings called *seraphs*. Each had six wings. Two of the wings covered their faces. Two covered their feet. And with the other two wings, they flew. The seraphs called to one another saying, "Holy, holy, holy is the LORD of hosts. The whole earth is filled with His glory!"

Instantly the doorposts shook and smoke filled the entire temple! (See **Isaiah** 6:4-5.) **Isaiah**, seeing and hearing all this, was terrified. Immediately he confessed his own sinfulness, crying, "Woe is me! [I am doomed to judgment!] I have sinful lips. The people I live among are sinful. I have seen with my eyes the King, the LORD Almighty."

Quickly a seraph, using tongs, grasped a burning coal from God's altar. (See **Isaiah** 6:6-7.) The seraph touched **Isaiah's** lips with the coal, saying, "Your sins are forgiven." God heard **Isaiah's** confession and forgave his sin.

Then the Lord asked, "Whom shall I send as a messenger to My people? Who will go for Us?" (**Isaiah** 6:8).

Promptly **Isaiah** answered: "Here am I. Send me!"

The Lord commanded, "Go, **Isaiah**. Urge My people to turn back to Me." But God added this warning: "My people will not listen to you, **Isaiah**." (See **Isaiah** 6:9-10.) Think of it! God was sending **Isaiah** to people who would ignore God's message. Do you think **Isaiah** decided, *I shall not be God's messenger*? Oh, no! He preached and taught and warned for about 50 years. (The next 60 chapters of his book record what he said.)

He also spoke many marvelous prophecies. Some of those prophecies have already been fulfilled. Others will yet come true in future years.

3. GOD'S PROMISE OF A SAVIOR
Isaiah 7:1-15; 9:6-7

An amazing prophecy recorded in **Isaiah** was about Someone who would come to earth. (Have students read aloud **Isaiah** 7:14.)

Show Illustration #3

God promised that a virgin (a pure, unmarried woman) would give birth to a Son. God Himself would be His Father. This was a miracle only God could do. His Son would be named "Immanuel." (*Teacher:* On dotted line at top of illustration, print IMMANUEL.) Immanuel is a name we do not often hear. But the people of Judah knew the marvelous meaning of this name. It is, *God with us*. (*Teacher:* Under IMMANUEL on illustration, print GOD WITH US.)

Are you wondering of whom the prophet spoke? Open your Bible to Matthew, the first book of the New Testament. Matthew wrote God's message 700 years after **Isaiah's** prophecy. (*Teacher:* If your students have Bibles, let them follow as you slowly read Matthew 1:18-23.)

Who was the virgin about whom **Isaiah** prophesied? (*Mary*.) What was to be the name of the Baby? (*Jesus*, Matthew 1:21.) What would Jesus do? (*Save His people from their sins*, Matthew 1:21.) **Isaiah** the *prophet* had told of another name for this Baby. What was that? (*Immanuel*, **Isaiah** 7:14; compare Matthew 1:22-23.) What does Immanuel mean? (*God with us*.)

(*Teacher:* Have students print in their notebooks the name *Immanuel* and its meaning: *God with us*.)

Isaiah prophesied again about this One who would come. Turn in your Bible to **Isaiah** 9:6. "For to us a child is born, to us a Son is given . . . He will be: the Wonderful [supernatural] Counselor; the Mighty God [He will conquer the evil one]; the Everlasting Father [He is forever the Father of His children]; the Prince of Peace [He gives peace to those who belong to Him]."

Isaiah prophesied these marvelous truths of Jesus long before He was born. But why did Jesus have to come to earth? Listen!

4. GOD'S PROVISION OF SALVATION
Isaiah 52:1-53:12

(*Teacher:* If you have a *Ryrie Study Bible* carefully read the excellent notes covering this important section of Scripture.)

Isaiah recorded this sad prophecy: "His face was so marred [so disfigured], He could hardly be recognized. He is despised and rejected . . . He was wounded . . . bruised . . . punished." (See **Isaiah** 52:14; 53:3, 5.)

Whose face was marred? Who was despised and rejected? Why was He wounded and bruised?

Show Illustration #4

From the New Testament we learn that **Isaiah** had prophesied of God's Son, the Lord Jesus Christ. (Point to illustration #4a.) Men spat on Him (Matthew 26:67). They struck Him with their fists (illustration #4b). With their hands (illustration #4c) they slapped His face (Matthew 26:67; John 18:22). They lashed Him (illustration #4d) with a whip (Matthew 27:26). With a reed (illustration #4e) they hit Him on His head (Matthew 27:30). Finally they crucified Him (Matthew 27:35). (*Teacher:* Around the shaded area on the illustration, draw a heavy line revealing top of cross.)

Why did Jesus take this awful punishment? **Isaiah's** prophecy tells the answer. "He was wounded for our transgressions [our sins]. He was bruised [crushed] for our iniquities [every wrong] . . . and with His stripes, we are healed [forgiven of our sin]." Why was Christ's awful suffering necessary? Because "all we like sheep have gone astray. We have turned every one to his own way." Turning from God to go our own way, is sin. And sin must be punished. Instead of punishing each of us, God did something we can hardly understand. God laid on the Lord Jesus "the iniquity [sin] of us all." (See **Isaiah** 53:5-6.)

(*Teacher:* Place a rock on a student's outstretched hand.) To help us understand what **Isaiah** said, we shall let this rock represent sin. We all have sinned. Our sin is like a heavy weight. Each one of us has turned from God and gone our own sinful way. But God laid on Christ, God's Anointed One, the sin of each one of us.

Now let us say that my Bible represents Christ. I shall ask (name student) to place his sin-rock on my Bible. Now, where is his sin? It is laid on Christ, the perfect One. Christ did not die because of His own sins, for He had none. Christ died for your sins and mine. He was wounded for *your* transgressions and bruised for *your* iniquities. Have you truly trusted in Christ as your Savior from sin? If so, He has forgiven your sin. If you have not trusted Him, will you place your trust in Him right now? Thank Him for dying for your sins. Ask Him for His forgiveness. (*Teacher:* Allow time for silent prayer.)

If you have truly asked the Lord to forgive your sin, will you tell me so after class?

Lesson 2
JEREMIAH AND LAMENTATIONS: MESSIAH'S UNBELIEVING PEOPLE

NOTE TO THE TEACHER

Jeremiah has been called the "prophet of tears." He wept because the Jewish people rebelled against the warnings of God. Jeremiah was born into a family of priests. He had been taught that God is holy. He knew the need of trusting and obeying the Lord.

Jeremiah lived through the Babylonian siege and destruction of Jerusalem. Instead of being taken to Babylon, he remained with the poor in Judah. Later he was forced to go with some rebels who went to Egypt. There he probably died. His ministry lasted more than 40 years.

Jeremiah sternly warned the people of Judah to: (1) forsake idol-worship; (2) repent of their sins and (3) return to the Lord. When the Jews would not repent, *Jeremiah* warned of the Babylonian captivity.

During all of *Jeremiah's* lifetime (through the reign of five kings), there were many national problems. Both Egypt and Babylon threatened God's people. Jeremiah continually warned the Jews of judgment. He also encouraged them with prophecies of the coming of Messiah. (See *Jeremiah* 23:5-8; 30:4-11; 31:31-34; 33:15-18.)

Like *Isaiah*, *Jeremiah* did not mention the name Messiah. He spoke of Him as: (1) the King from David's family; and (2) the Righteous Branch from David's family.

Scripture to be studied: Jeremiah 1:1-33:26; 37:1-39:18; Lamentations 1:1-5:22

The *aim* of the lesson: To teach the seriousness of disobeying God.

What your students should *know*: God must punish the sin of those who do not believe Him.

What your students should *feel*: A keen desire to he true to the Lord always.

What your students should *do*: Be obedient to God, even if others are against them.

Lesson outline (for the teacher's and students' notebooks):
1. Sins of Judah (Jeremiah 1:1-20:18).
2. Punishment of Judah (Jeremiah 21:1-29:32).
3. Destruction of Jerusalem (Jeremiah 37:1-39:18; Lamentations 1:1-5:22).
4. Promises for Future (Jeremiah 30:1-33:26).

The verse to be memorized:

Obey My voice, and I will be your God, and ye shall be my people: and walk ye in all the ways that I have commanded you, that it may be well unto you. (Jeremiah 7:23)

THE LESSON

Did you ever see a young man cry? What made him cry? (*Teacher:* Encourage student response.)

God's prophet, young **Jeremiah**, became known as "the crying [weeping] prophet." (See **Jeremiah** 9:1; 13:17;

Lamentations 1:16; 2:11-12; 3:48-51.) Prophets spoke for God. What could cause a prophet to cry? Listen carefully.

1. SINS OF JUDAH
Jeremiah 1:1-20:18

God had told **Jeremiah**, "Long before you were born, I set you apart. I have chosen you to be a prophet to the nations." (See **Jeremiah** 1:5.)

"O Lord God," **Jeremiah** answered, "I do not know how to speak."

God said, "Do not say that. Go wherever I send you and say what I command you. Do not be afraid. I am with you and shall take care of you." (See **Jeremiah** 1:4-10.)

Many years earlier God had told the Jews, "I have chosen you to be My special people." (See Deuteronomy 7:6.) God promised them good if they would obey Him. He also warned of punishment if they disobeyed. But again and again God's people in Judah disobeyed Him. They turned from the true God and worshiped idols they themselves made. (See **Jeremiah** 1:16.) So **Jeremiah** was to tell the people of Judah that God would punish them. Thinking of giving this message to God's people made **Jeremiah** cry.

Through **Jeremiah** God warned, "A nation from the north [Babylon] is coming." (*Teacher:* Using the back cover map of Old Testament Volume #26 of this series, show locations of Judah and Babylon.) **Jeremiah** continued, "The men of Babylon are cruel. They will ride horses and attack with bows and spears." (See **Jeremiah** 1:14-16; 4:6; 6:1, 22-25; 10:22; 13:20.)

Do you think the people of Judah turned back to God when they heard His message? No, they did not! The people God had chosen for Himself, did not believe God. This made **Jeremiah** so sad, he wanted to cry day and night. (See **Jeremiah** 9:1.)

So God told **Jeremiah**, "Go buy a linen belt. Wear it around your waist close to your body." Immediately **Jeremiah** obeyed. (See **Jeremiah** 13:1-14.)

After awhile God commanded, "Now take off that linen belt. Hide it among the rocks." **Jeremiah** did as he was told.

Later, God ordered, "**Jeremiah**, go get that linen belt."

Show Illustration #5

When **Jeremiah** dug out the belt, it was ruined and useless. God sighed, saying, "As a belt is bound around a man's waist, so I bound all My people to Myself. I wanted them to praise and honor Me. But they have not listened." (See **Jeremiah** 13:11.)

Then God made a stern announcement. "As that belt was destroyed, so I shall destroy Judah and its capital city, Jerusalem. The people of Judah are proud and wicked. They stubbornly refuse to obey Me. They bow down to idols and are completely useless to Me. So I shall destroy them." (See **Jeremiah** 13:14.) **Jeremiah** understood that God's people did not believe God's warning. For this, they would be taken as captives to another land. "When this happens," **Jeremiah** said, "my eyes shall overflow with tears." (See **Jeremiah** 13:17.)

The Lord continued to warn His people. (See **Jeremiah** 14:1-15:2; 16:1-4.) Still they did not believe Him, so their sins became worse. They even sacrificed their children to idols! (See **Jeremiah** 19:1-6.)

Finally, God announced through **Jeremiah**: "I shall give all Judah to the king of Babylon! He will carry away My people to his country. Many will be killed. I shall hand over to the enemy king all the treasures of Jerusalem. Everything will be taken to Babylon." (See **Jeremiah** 20:4-5.)

God would give His people and everything valuable to the enemy. God loved His people and had warned them of His punishment. Yet they did not believe Him. Not to believe God is sin. And sin must be punished.

2. PUNISHMENT OF JUDAH
Jeremiah 21:1-29:32

Soon two of the king's men rushed to **Jeremiah**. "Ask the Lord to help us!" they begged. "King Nebuchadnezzar of Babylon and his army are marching against us. Ask the Lord to do a miracle for us! He can send Nebuchadnezzar back to Babylon!"

Show Illustration #6A

Jeremiah answered, "The Lord God says, 'I am about to turn against you. I Myself shall fight against you . . . I shall strike down men and animals living in Jerusalem . . . I shall hand over your king and all the people to Nebuchadnezzar, king of Babylon. He will destroy My people by the sword. He will not show them mercy or pity.'" (See **Jeremiah** 21:1-7.) The people of Judah had turned from God and had to be punished. Even the priests and leaders of the nation had disobeyed the Lord. (See **Jeremiah** 2:8; 10:21; 23:1-2.) So everyone–including those who led God's people–would receive His punishment.

Suddenly, after all the bad news, there was good news!

Show Illustration #6B

Through **Jeremiah** the Lord declared: "The days are coming when I shall raise up a King. He will be from David's family . . . In His days Judah will be saved." (See **Jeremiah** 23:5-6.)

Were God's people happy to learn about a King who will come? We are not told. But you and I are glad to hear it. For this wonderful prophecy is about Christ, God's Anointed One. (*Teacher:* Show poster on back cover.) He is the One God anointed to rule over the earth some future day.

Jeremiah told the people of Judah, "For 23 years I have warned you to turn from your evil ways. Now listen to what God says: 'I shall call King Nebuchadnezzar of Babylon to come against Judah and the surrounding nations. I shall completely destroy all of them. And you, My people, and the people of nearby nations, will serve the king of Babylon for 70 years'." (See **Jeremiah** 25:8-11.)

So God would hand over His own people to the heathen Babylonians! And God's people would be captives in a foreign land for 70 years! Think of that!

3. DESTRUCTION OF JERUSALEM
Jeremiah 37:1-39:18; Lamentations 1:1-5:22

(*Teacher:* Study also 2 Kings 24:18-25:21; **Jeremiah** 52:1-30.)

Exactly as God had warned, King Nebuchadnezzar and his army marched to Jerusalem. They camped around the city walls. And for two years none of God's people could leave the city. At last there was no food, so the people of Judah were starving.

Finally the Babylonians rushed into Jerusalem. They set fire to God's magnificent temple, the beautiful palace, and all the houses. Every building in Jerusalem was ablaze. (See **Jeremiah** 52:1-30.) Nebuchadnezzar's soldiers stole the gold, silver, and bronze treasures. All these had been used in the temple where the true God was worshiped. Now everything was going to Babylon where it would be used for idol-worship.

Show Illustration #7

Then the Babylonian soldiers seized the people of Judah amid marched them as slaves to Babylon. (See **Jeremiah** 52:27b-30.) Only the poor and weak were left behind.

The people of Judah had turned from God to worship man-made idols. So God allowed them to be prisoners of Babylonian idol-worshipers!

Jeremiah sat alone looking at the ruins of Jerusalem. Oh, how sad he was! In his sadness, he wrote five poems. These have been kept for us in the Bible book of Lamentations.

Jeremiah began: "How lonely is the city which was filled with people . . . Once she was great among the nations. Now she has become a slave." (See Lamentations 1:1.) "Jerusalem remembers the treasures which were once hers. Now her enemies look at her and laugh because she was destroyed." (See Lamentations 1:7.)

Jeremiah sobbed, "Is there any suffering like my suffering? . . . My eyes overflow with tears." (Lamentations 1:12, 16). He knew that God had allowed the beautiful city to be destroyed. So **Jeremiah** groaned, "The Lord swallowed up all the houses . . . He swallowed the people. He has swallowed the palace . . . The Lord has destroyed the magnificent temple where He met with His people. He has handed the king's beautiful palace to the enemy." (See Lamentations2:1-2, 5, 7.)

Jeremiah cried, "The children are also captured by Babylon" (Lamentations 1:5). For the poor ones left behind, **Jeremiah** begged, "Even in the night, pray to the Lord for the children who are starving in the street . . . See the babies– each one so thirsty its tongue sticks to the roof of its mouth. Children beg for bread, but no one gives it to them." (See Lamentations 2:11, 19; 4:4. *Teacher:* Observe the awfulness recorded in Lamentations 4:10. No wonder **Jeremiah** wept!)

Sadly **Jeremiah** added, "The Lord has done what He planned" (Lamentations 2:17). The people had willfully, sinfully turned away from God. And sin must be punished. This time God used the heathen of Babylon to punish His own dear people.

Suddenly **Jeremiah** exclaimed, "But I have hope! It is because of the Lord's faithful love that we are not totally destroyed. His love never fails. It is new every morning. Great is Your faithfulness, O Lord." (See Lamentations 3:21-26.)

So **Jeremiah** dried his tears.

4. PROMISES FOR FUTURE
Jeremiah 30:1-33:26

One day the Lord gave a wonderful promise to **Jeremiah**. "A day is coming," God said, "when I shall bring my captive people (both Israel and Judah) back to this land. I gave this land to their ancestors. And some day My people will have it again." (See **Jeremiah** 30:3; 31:16-17, 27-28.)

"In that coming day," God said, "I shall make a new agreement [*covenant*] with My people (Israel and Judah). I shall write My Law in their hearts. I shall he their God and they will be My people. All My people will know Me. And I shall take away their sins." (See **Jeremiah** 31:31-34; 32:37-44; Ezekiel 37:21-28; Romans 11:26-27; Hebrews 8:6-12.)

God again spoke of the day which is yet to come. He said, "I shall cause a Righteous Branch to come from David's family. He will rule wisely. He will do only right. He will never make a mistake. The days of all wicked kings and rulers will be over." (See **Jeremiah** 33:14-17.) Who is "the Righteous Branch from David's family?" *Christ, God's anointed One*. He was born a baby here on earth where He lived for 33 years. Then He died on the cross taking the punishment for our sins. He arose from the dead and ascended to heaven where He is now. But a day will come when all God's prophecies through **Jeremiah** will finally come true.

In that "coming day" (of which **Jeremiah** prophesied), Christ, God's Anointed One (show back cover poster) will come again to earth.

Show Illustration #8

Then Christ will sit on a throne in Jerusalem. There He will reign for 1,000 years, always doing right. (See **Isaiah** 11:1-12; 66:10-14; **Micah** 4:1-3.) and God's people will gladly, lovingly obey Him.

But what about *you* today? Do you gladly, lovingly obey the Lord? If not, will you ask Him right now to forgive you? Then ask for His help as you seek to obey Him today–and in the days ahead. (*Teacher:* Allow time for silent prayer.)

Lesson 3
EZEKIEL: GOD'S GLORY AND VICTORY

NOTE TO THE TEACHER

There are many Bible references included here for your careful study. Only then will you be able to teach with authority the tremendous truths of *Ezekiel's* prophecies.

The glory of God was the hope and power of *Ezekiel's* ministry. God's glory shows His greatness, His worthiness, His splendor, His majesty, His honor, His excellence. While teaching this lesson, refer often to God's glory.

There is enough material here for three or four teaching sessions. Make the marvelous truths live! And remember: a law of good teaching is review, REVIEW, REVIEW!

To review lesson #2, use illustrations #6a and #7 to discuss *why* and *how* God punished His people.

With illustrations #6b and #8, recount *Jeremiah's* prophecy of the King, the Righteous Branch from David's family, who will come to reign over the earth.

BACKGROUND

Ezekiel was taken from Jerusalem to Babylonia (in 597 B.C.) with thousands of upper class citizens. (See 2 Kings 24:14-17.) All were settled near the city of Nippur, southeast of Babylon.

Ezekiel was called to be a prophet when he was about 30 years old. He ministered for approximately 22 years.

Ezekiel had two emphases in his messages: (1) God's glory and reign over His people and (2) God's restoration of His people after the Tribulation. (At that time, the Millennium [1,000 years] of blessing, will begin. Christ will then rule over the world sitting on David's throne in Jerusalem.)

Ezekiel's messages were comforting. He prophesied that: (1) God's people will some day be restored to their homeland; (2) God's people will have a glorious new temple; and (3) God's people will truly turn to Him.

Throughout *Ezekiel's* ministry, God's glory and supreme power are most important. (See, for example, Ezekiel 1:4, 26-28; 3:12, 23; 8:4; 9:3; 10:4, 18; 11:22- 23; 43:2-4; 44:4; 48:35.)

Like *Isaiah* and *Jeremiah*, *Ezekiel* does not mention the name Messiah. Instead he speaks of Him, saying, "My Servant, David . . . will be King over My people." (See Ezekiel 37:24; compare Luke 1:32.)

NOTE: All Scripture references in the lesson text are from the book of *Ezekiel* unless otherwise stated.

Scripture to be studied: Ezekiel 8:1-9:3; 10:4-19; 11:22-25; 28:1-19; 34:1-38:23

The *aim* of the lesson: To give an understanding of God's glory.

What your students should *know*: That God will punish those who sin.

What your students should *feel*: Awe and reverence for the glory of God who wants to be with His people.

What your students should *do*: Trust Christ for salvation and resist Satan's temptations.

Lesson outline (for the teacher's and students' notebooks):
1. God's glory leaves His temple (Ezekiel 8:1-11:25).
2. God's victory for His people (Ezekiel 37:1-28).
3. God's victory over Satan (Ezekiel 28:1-19).
4. God's glory in His Kingdom (Ezekiel 34:1-38:23).

The verse to be memorized:

And I will make them one nation in the land . . . and one King shall be King to them all . . . [I] will cleanse them . . . and I will be their God. (Ezekiel 37:22-23)

THE LESSON

Today we learn of another of God's great prophets–**Ezekiel**. What is a prophet and what did a prophet do? (Encourage student response.) Prophets were chosen by God. They were to tell His people what the Lord would do in the future. Some prophecies were filled with wonderful promises for God's people. Many of the prophecies warned of punishment for sinning against God.

We have learned about two (2) prophets in these lessons. What are their names? (**Isaiah** and **Jeremiah**.)

The prophet **Ezekiel** lived at the same time as **Jeremiah**. **Jeremiah** had warned the Jews to repent of their sins and turn to God. If they would not do so, another country would conquer Judah. Most people did not listen to **Jeremiah**. Because of this, God allowed King Nebuchadnezzar of Babylon to march against Jerusalem. He captured many Jews and took them to Babylon (known today as *Iraq*). Young **Ezekiel** was one of those prisoners.

In *Jerusalem*, **Jeremiah** continued prophesying to the Jews who had not been captured. **Ezekiel** became God's prophet to the captive Jews in *Babylon*. (See 2:1-7.) **Ezekiel** was also a priest. (See 1:3.) A priest prayed to God for the people and their needs. He offered sacrifices for the sins of the people. **Ezekiel** was sad because most Jews felt as if they had never sinned. They did not bother to offer sacrifices to God. Nor did they ask God's forgiveness for their sins. (See 3:7; 5:5-6, 11.)

1. GOD'S GLORY LEAVES HIS TEMPLE
Ezekiel 8:1-11:25

Hundreds of years before **Ezekiel** lived, God's people (the Jews) had escaped from Egypt. Do you remember the name of the one who led them? (*Moses*). The Jews wandered through the desert towards the land God had promised them. On their way (at Mount Sinai) God directed Moses to build a tabernacle (a movable tent). At the tabernacle, God met with His people. The most important part of the tabernacle was the Holy of Holies. (It was sometimes called the Most Holy Place. See, for example, Numbers 18:10.) Only the High Priest could go into the Most Holy Place. And he could go in only once each year (on the Day of Atonement–see Leviticus 16:2, 34; Hebrews 9:7).

Do you know why the Holy of Holies was a very special place? It is because the "glory of God" (His very own brightness) shone there. (See Exodus 25:22, 40:34-35.) God's glory was so bright that no one could look at it. Have you ever tried to look straight into the sun? (Do not do it! For the brightness could blind you.) The glory of God was even brighter than the sun! (See Acts 26:13.)

Years later, King Solomon obeyed God and built a magnificent temple in Jerusalem. (The temple replaced the tabernacle.) The temple became the place of worship for the Jews. And the glory of the LORD filled the temple. (See 1 Kings 8:11; 2 Chronicles 5:13-14.)

God's shining glory reminded His people that He was with them. God's glory showed His power, His perfection, and much more. How blessed the Jews were! All other religions worshiped man-made gods of wood and stone. But the Jewish people had God's glorious presence in their temple. Surely this should have made a difference in the way the Jews lived. And for years, many Jews did obey God. But by the time of **Ezekiel**, everything had changed.

One day God showed **Ezekiel** a vision, something like a dream. God sometimes gave messages to His prophets through visions. In **Ezekiel's** mind he saw a picture. He also heard God's words.

In the vision, God showed **Ezekiel** what was happening in God's holy temple. **Ezekiel** saw man-made idols in the temple. (See 8:5, 10.) He saw terrible drawings covering the walls. And God's own people were worshiping the idols and the drawings! (See 8:5-12.) Other Jews, instead of worshiping God, were worshiping the sun which God had created. (See 8:16.)

How do you suppose the Lord God felt about this? (Let students discuss.) God was angry! He hated what His people were doing. (See 8:17-18.) God said He would not pity His people. Nor would He spare them. He would punish them severely! (See 9:10.)

Show Illustration #9

In the vision, **Ezekiel** saw the glory of God move. First, God's glory left the Holy of Holies. (See 10:18.) God would not stay where man-made idols and horrid drawings were worshiped.

As **Ezekiel** watched, God's glorious brightness kept moving. (See 10:19.) Finally it was outside the temple and disappeared entirely. God's glory was gone. He had turned away from His people whom He dearly loved. Why? Because they had turned against Him. What a sad day for the people of God!

Now please listen carefully. Most of the Jews did not even care that God had gone! It made no difference to them. Why? Because they had sinned against God.

Here is something you should never forget. God will finally punish all those who have never trusted the Lord Jesus Christ to save them from their sins. They will be separated from God forever. (*Teacher:* Read John 3:36.) And forever they will suffer in hell. (See Revelation 20:11-15.)

Have you truly trusted in Jesus Christ, God the Son? If so, your sins have been forgiven. If you have not believed in Christ, please talk to me about this after class.

The time came when the Jews were captured and taken from their homeland. God's very own people were scattered among other nations. But God had given many wonderful promises to His people. What happened to those promises?

To answer this question, God gave another vision to **Ezekiel**.

2. GOD'S VICTORY FOR HIS PEOPLE
Ezekiel 37:1-28

In this vision, the Spirit of God led **Ezekiel** into a valley. No one else was there. It was deathly quiet. (See 37:1-10.)

Looking about, **Ezekiel** saw the valley was covered with very dry bones. He walked back and forth across the valley. But everywhere he went he saw only dead bones–stacks of them. The hot sun had made them dry and brittle. (*Teacher:* If you have New Testament Volume #22 of this series, see lesson #4, points #1 and #2.)

God asked, "**Ezekiel**, can these bones live?"

"O LORD God," **Ezekiel** answered, "You alone know if they can live."

Then God commanded, "**Ezekiel**, prophesy to the dry bones. Tell them I shall make them live again. They will come together. I shall put flesh on the bones and cover them with skin."

Now put yourself in **Ezekiel's** place. Would you have been willing to prophesy to dead bones? (Encourage student response.)

Show Illustration #10

Ezekiel obeyed God perfectly and prophesied to the bones. Suddenly there were rattling noises all over the valley! The bones came together! They attached to each other exactly as they had been. They were people! But they did not move. There was no breath in them.

God then caused the wind to blow and He breathed into each body. The people came to life. They stood up–a huge crowd!

Then God told the meaning of the vision. He said, "**Ezekiel**, these bones are like My people, the Jews. They are scattered among other nations. (Many were then in Assyria, some in Egypt, others in Babylon.) Because My people sinned, they are like dead, scattered bones. They are saying, 'We have no hope'."

God continued, "Now, **Ezekiel**, prophesy to My people. Tell them what I am going to do. Some day I shall gather My people from among the nations. I shall bring them back to Israel, their own land. My people–of Israel and Judah–will again be one nation." (See 34:11-16.)

What a wonderful promise for the Jews! They had turned away from God many times. But He would love them forever.

God's promise of gathering all the Jews has not yet come true. Thousands are spread throughout the world. Many do not care about God. Most do not believe that the Lord Jesus Christ is God's Son. But one day God will miraculously bring them back together in their homeland. There He will give them true faith in Him. And then they will trust in Christ, God's dear Son.

3. GOD'S VICTORY OVER SATAN
Ezekiel 28:1-19

Do you wonder why this has not yet happened? Why has it taken so long for God's people to return to their homeland? There is someone who is against the Jews returning to their own land. He does not want them to receive God's blessings. Who is always against God's plans? Who is God's great enemy? (*Satan*)

Satan was not always the enemy of God. From the book of **Ezekiel** we learn that Satan was created by God. He was perfect, beautiful, and very wise. (God compared him to the very wealthy, proud king of Tyre. See 28:1-2.) God chose Satan to guard the throne of God. (See 28:12-15a.)

But one day Satan became proud. He wanted to be like God. He wanted to be worshiped as God is worshiped. (See 28:15b-17; **Isaiah** 14:12-15.) So Satan had sinned. And God, the holy One, could not permit sin in Heaven.

Show Illustration #11

God punished this one beautiful angel–Satan–by hurling him out of heaven. Ever since, Satan has hated God. He hates all the good plans of God. He does everything he can to keep people from believing in Christ. Satan deceives people. He causes them to disobey God.

So far, Satan has kept most Jews out of their homeland. But God is all powerful. (See 1 John 4:4.) The Lord is able to have all the Jews return to their land. And He will do so–in His time.

4. GOD'S GLORY IN HIS KINGDOM
Ezekiel 34:1-38:23

God spoke again to **Ezekiel**. He said, "Tell My people that I shall gather them to their homeland. They will come from all over the world. Then, in their homeland, they will be safe and live in peace."

God continued with a particularly wonderful promise. He said, "I shall give My people, the Jews, a new heart. I shall put My Spirit in them. Then they will obey My laws and do as I command" (36:26-27).

The Lord also promised, "I shall cleanse My people from their sins. Their land will be rebuilt. They will have plenty of food from their fields and trees. Their land will be like the Garden of Eden (prosperous, peaceful, beautiful). And My people will know that I am the LORD." (See 36:33-38.)

God then added a most glorious promise. He said, "David My servant shall be your king," (37:24-25). Years before, God had made a promise to King David. The LORD told him, "One from your family will reign forever." (See 2 Samuel 7:12-16.) Many descendants of David's family were not faithful to God. Some even became idolators.

However, one day David's greatest descendant will return to the earth. Who is David's greatest descendant? (*The Lord Jesus Christ*) The Messiah–Christ is God's Anointed One will save His people, the Jews. (Show back cover poster.)

Show Illustration #8

Christ will reign on earth from His throne in Jerusalem for 1,000 years. (See 37:21-28.) These 1,000 years are known as *The Millennium* or *The Millennial Kingdom*.

God gave **Ezekiel** another vision. He showed him the temple which will be built in the future Millennium. (Remember, this has not yet happened!) God told **Ezekiel** exactly how the temple will look. (See 40:1-43:27.) As **Ezekiel** watched, he saw in the vision something amazing.

Show Illustration #12

The glory of the LORD came down and filled that future temple! (See 43:1-4.) Seeing this, **Ezekiel** fell to the ground and worshiped God. (See 44:4.) In that future day God will again dwell with His people, the Jews. He will be their God and they shall be His own dear people. God says all the nations will then know that He is the LORD. They will know He has chosen the Jewish people for His special blessings. (See 37:26-28.)

Ezekiel's prophecies give hope to the Jewish people. God will never forget them, for He chose them for Himself. But one day God will miraculously bring them all back to Israel, the land He chose for them. There He will give them true faith in Himself. And then they will trust in Christ, God's dear Son.

In the meantime, every person who has received Christ as Savior has a marvelous hope. At any time–it could be today!– Jesus Christ will come in the air. He will catch up all His own and take them with Him to heaven. (See John 14:1-6; 1 Corinthians 15:51-52; 1 Thessalonians 4:13-18.) There they will see God's glory forever.

Anyone can be a part of God's glorious future. But we all (Jews and Gentiles) must receive Christ, God's Anointed One. If you have not trusted in Him, will you do so right now? I shall gladly talk with you about this if you remain after class.

Lesson 4
DANIEL: GOD RULES OVER ALL

Scripture to be studied: Daniel 4:1-37; 7:1-28; 9:1-27; 12:1-13; Revelation 19:11-22:21

The *aim* of the lesson: To prove that God rules over all–people and nations.

What your students should *know*: That all God's prophecies will come true–in His time.

What your students should *feel*: Assured that God always does right.

What your students should *do*: Believe God's prophecies and promises. Purpose to do God's will each day.

Lesson outline (for the teacher's and students' notebooks):

1. God's rule over rulers (Daniel 4:1-37).
2. God's rule over governments (Daniel 7:1-28).
3. God's rule over Israel (Daniel 9:1-27).
4. God's rule over earth (Daniel 12:1-13; Revelation 19:11-22:21).

The verse to be memorized:

The Most High ruleth in the kingdom of men, and giveth it to whomsoever He will. (Daniel 4:32b)

THE LESSON

For many years God's people, the Jews, worshiped idols instead of God. God's prophets warned His people to repent and return to the Lord. But the people sinfully refused to do so.

They were guilty also of another sin. God had commanded His people to let their land rest every seventh year. They were to plant and harvest for six years. But the seventh year the land was to have rest. God promised they would have plenty to eat during that seventh year. (See Leviticus 25:2-7.)

But for 490 years God's people refused to obey Him. They planted their fields every year–including each seventh year. (*Teacher:* Show on chalkboard: 490 years divided by 7th

[year] equals 70 [years].) This means that during those 490 years, there were 70 years when the fields should have lain idle. But God's people never obeyed His command. Would He punish His people for this? Yes, He surely would! God allowed them to be captives in Babylon for 70 years. For those 70 years, their land had its rest. (See 2 Chronicles 36:20-21.)

God had not punished His people without warning them. (See **Jeremiah** 25:11.) **Daniel**, the prophet, had studied **Jeremiah's** prophecies. So he wrote, "I, **Daniel**, understand the Scriptures. According to the word of the LORD given to the prophet **Jeremiah**, Jerusalem will be desolate (*empty; forsaken*) for 70 years." (See **Daniel** 9:2.) **Daniel** knew what all God's people should have known. The Jews would be out of their homeland for 70 years. For what reason? They had not let their land have rest. They had disobeyed God.

The Lord warned His people. But He also gave them this wonderful promise: "When 70 years are completed in Babylon, I shall come to you. And I shall bring you back to your land. I have plans for you, My people." (See **Jeremiah** 29:10-11.)

Daniel and his friends were young when King Nebuchadnezzar captured them. (See **Daniel** 1:1-6.) Imagine how they felt, knowing they would be in a foreign land for 70 years!

God had a wonderful surprise for Daniel and three of his friends. (See **Daniel** 2:48-49; 3:30.) These four were chosen to serve in King Nebuchadnezzar's court. There they would be taught. They were even placed in charge of some of the king's affairs!

1. GOD'S RULE OVER RULERS
Daniel 4:1-37

Some years later, King Nebuchadnezzar had a dream. And he was afraid! In his dream he saw a giant tree reaching up to heaven. But the great tree was cut down. Nebuchadnezzar called his wise men. "Tell me the meaning of my dream," he demanded. But the wise men shook their heads. They did not understand what the dream meant.

Show Illustration #13A

King Nebuchadnezzar called for Daniel. "I had a dream," the king began. "I want you to tell me what it means. I saw a huge tree. Its top reached the sky. It could be seen all over the earth. There was fruit on the tree–enough for everyone. The beasts of the field found shelter under the tree. And the birds lived in its branches. From the tree, everyone was fed." (See **Daniel** 4:9-12.)

Almost in a whisper, the king added, "Suddenly I saw in my dream an angel-like being from heaven. He called, 'Cut down the tree! Take off its branches! Shake off the leaves! Scatter its fruit! Let the animals get away from under it! Let the birds fly away from its branches! Let the stump and its roots be bound! . . . Let him live with the animals . . . Let his mind be changed from that of a man . . . Let him have the mind of an animal . . .'" (See **Daniel** 4:13-16.)

When **Daniel** heard the dream, he was troubled. But finally he had courage to tell the meaning of the dream. "You, O king, are that tree! You have become great and strong. Your greatness reaches the sky . . . But you, O king, will be sent away from people. You will live like the wild animals. You will eat grass like cattle. . . . You will be like that until you know the Most High (God) reigns over all kingdoms. And He gives those kingdoms to whomever He wishes . . . You will receive your kingdom again only when you admit that God rules over everything–and everyone. So, O king, please take my advice. Turn from your sins. Do what is right." (See **Daniel** 4:22-27.)

Nebuchadnezzar listened to everything **Daniel** said. But he did nothing about it.

A year later, he took a walk on the roof of his royal palace. He admired the city of Babylon. Proudly he exclaimed, "Is not this the great Babylon which I built?"

Immediately a voice spoke to him from heaven. "This is what will happen to you, King Nebuchadnezzar. Your kingdom is taken from you. You will live with the wild animals. You will eat grass like cattle until you admit that the Most High (God) is over all kingdoms."

Show Illustration #13B

At that very moment Nebuchadnezzar was forced away from people. He ate grass like cattle. His body was wet with dew. His hair grew like feathers on an eagle. His nails were like claws of a bird. (See **Daniel** 4:28-33.)

Finally, after a long time, Nebuchadnezzar looked up to heaven. He began to think right. Then he worshiped the Lord, saying, "I praise the Most High (God). He lives forever. He rules over everything. His kingdom lasts forever . . . He does according to His will . . . Now I, Nebuchadnezzar, praise the King of heaven. Everything He does is right. All His ways are right. And those who are proud, He humbles." (See **Daniel** 4:34-37.)

The king had learned his lesson. God rules over all rulers, even Nebuchadnezzar.

2. GOD'S RULE OVER GOVERNMENTS
Daniel 7:1-28

When **Daniel** was about age 70, Nebuchadnezzar died. And Belshazzar became the new king of Babylon. At this time, God caused **Daniel** to have a frightening dream. In the morning **Daniel** wrote about this God-given dream. (See **Daniel** 7:1-8.)

Show Illustration #14

"In my night-vision," **Daniel** wrote, "I saw four great beasts. One was like a strong lion (Point to 14A.) with speedy eagles' wings. The second beast looked like a fierce bear clutching three ribs in its teeth (Point to 14B). The third beast seemed to be a 4-headed leopard (Point to 14C.) with four wings. The fourth beast was dreadful to see. It had 10 horns (Point to 14D.) and a little horn with eyes and a mouth." (See **Daniel** 7:4-8.)

Daniel saw more. He wrote, "I saw the Judge of all the earth (God–*the Ancient of Days*). His clothing was white as snow. (Point to 14E.) The hair on His head was like white wool. His throne was like flaming fire." (See **Daniel** 7:9-10.)

Daniel wondered what it all meant. He asked and was told: "The four great beasts are four kings" who will reign over earth's kingdom. (See **Daniel** 7:17.)

It would not have been hard for **Daniel** to understand this. He could never forget how Nebuchadnezzar, king of Babylon, captured him with the other Jews. Nebuchadnezzar had been like a strong lion with speedy eagles' wings. (Point to 14a) He tore God's people from Jerusalem and led them as prisoners of war to Babylon.

NOTE TO THE TEACHER

Please study this material carefully.

Young *Daniel* was one of the captives taken by King Nebuchadnezzar to Babylon. There, among idol-worshipers, *Daniel* honored the living God. And God honored *Daniel*. (See *Daniel* 1:5-9.) Through *Daniel*, God gave tremendous prophecies. Some are not easily understood. Do not be surprised. *Daniel* himself did not understand all the prophecies! (See *Daniel* 12:8.)

Daniel prophesied about 2,500 years ago. Many of his prophecies have already come true. Others are yet to be fulfilled–in God's time. Throughout this major book of prophecy, God is seen ruling over everything and everyone.

Daniel's book is packed with many truths. Only a few are included in this lesson. Not included are two well-known events: The three young men in the fiery furnace, and *Daniel* in the lions' den. This latter narrative (with illustrations) appears in the VISUALIZED BIBLE series, New Testament volume #21, lesson #3. You could teach these dramatic accounts as an introductory lesson. Be sure to emphasize the spiritual qualities of these four young men.

Regarding lesson point #2: Study *Daniel* 2:27-44 along with *Daniel* 7:1-28. The second chapter of *Daniel* is not included in this lesson. But the prophecies are of same kings and kingdoms as in chapter seven. See below the comparative chart of Nebuchadnezzar's and *Daniel's* dreams.

If kings and kingdoms are terms not known to your students, here are suggested substitutes: Instead of *kingdom*–nation; country; empire; monarchy; tribe; government. Instead of *king*–emperor; prime . . . minister; premier; chief; monarch; president.

Regarding lesson point #3: In *Daniel* 9:24 the word "weeks" is used. In the Hebrew language (in this instance) the Old Testament word "weeks" means sevens. "Sevens" is used for groups of seven years. (Compare. Genesis 29:27-28; Leviticus 25:8.) Therefore the prophecy of seventy sevens of years equals 490 years. (70 multiplied by 7=490.) For your sake, Teacher, "sevens" are included in the lesson text. But for your students, only total numbers of years are needed.

At the close of section #3, mention is made of God's choosing Israel for Himself. For your own review, Teacher, read from this series Old Testament volume #6 entitled *Election*. Also helpful is New Testament volume #22, *God and Israel*.

Regarding lesson point #4: Included are some teachings from the book of Revelation. Not all the future events were revealed to *Daniel*. (See *Daniel* 12:8-13.) However, since the Bible closes with added details, a few are used here.

You will want to divide this text into two or more lessons.

To review *Ezekiel's* prophecy (lesson #3), encourage student participation.

With illustration #9, discuss the departure of God's glory from His temple.

Using illustration #10, make certain that students understand *Ezekiel's* dry bones vision: God will some day bring back the Jewish people to their homeland.

With illustration #12, students should tell of God's glory returning to God's temple during the future Millennial reign of Christ.

NEBUCHADNEZZAR'S AND DANIEL'S DREAMS

Refer to this chart when studying point #2 of lesson.

As you study, compare the teachings of *Daniel* 2:24-43 with *Daniel* 7:4.28. The statue in Nebuchadnezzar's dream and the beasts of which *Daniel* dreamed, teach the same truths. The chart below should be helpful to you. Whether or not you share it with your students, depends on their ages and abilities.

	Nebuchadnezzar's Dream	Interpretation (Kingdoms or Empires)	Daniel's Dream
1	Gold head Daniel 2:32a	BABYLON Daniel 2:37-38 Babylon conquers Judah (605 years before Christ)	First beast: lion / eagle Daniel 7:4
2	Silver chest and arms Daniel 2:32b	MEDO-PERSIA Daniel 2:39a Medo-persia conquers Babylon (538 years before Christ)	Second beast: bear Daniel 7:5 (See 9:1)
3	Bronze belly and thighs Daniel 2:32c	GREECE Daniel 2:39b Greece conquers Medo-Persia (333 years before Christ)	Third beast: leopard with 4 heads (Greece finally had 4 heads: Asia Minor; Syria; Egypt; Macedonia) Daniel 7:6
4	Iron legs and clay feet Daniel 2:33	ROME Daniel 2:40-43 Rome conquers Greece (63 years before Christ)	Fourth fierce beast with 10 horns plus 1 little horn Daniel 7:7-8, 23-24a

MAPS OF THESE EMPIRES APPEAR ON PAGE 38.

Now it was clear that another king (like a fierce beam–*Medo Persia*) would overtake the Babylonians. Later some other king (like a 4-headed leopard–*Greece*) would swallow the "fierce bear" king and his kingdom. Finally the king with 10 horns (the *Roman Empire*) and a little horn (anti-Christ), would overtake all the other kingdoms.

So **Daniel** understood that kingdoms would come and kingdoms will go. But God is always in control. He determines ahead of time when governments will begin. He knows when they will end. Nothing surprises Hum. For He rules forever over all the governments of all the world.

3. GOD'S RULE OVER ISRAEL
Daniel 9:1-27

Daniel (now about age 85) loved and obeyed the Lord. One day, while reading the Scriptures, he saw again something he knew. God had prophesied through the prophet **Jeremiah** that the city of Jerusalem would be empty (*desolate*) for 70 years. (See **Jeremiah** 29:10.) God had also promised, "When 70 years are completed in Babylon, I shall come to you. I have plans to prosper you. I shall bring you and all My people back from the places to which I carried you into exile." (See **Jeremiah** 29:11-14.)

Understanding this, **Daniel** turned at once to the Lord. He prayed, "O Lord, You keep your promises to all who love You and obey Your commands. We have sinned. We have rebelled against You and turned from Your commands. You have scattered us . . . because we have sinned. Nothing has ever been done like that which you did to Your city–Jerusalem. But we have not asked Your forgiveness. Nor have we turned back to You. We have sinned, we have done wrong. Hear, O God. Open Your eyes . . . see the desolation of Your city, Jerusalem. O Lord, forgive! For Your sake, O my God, answer quickly." (See **Daniel** 9:1-19.)

Immediately the angel Gabriel came to **Daniel** with a message. He said, "As soon as you began to pray, God answered. I have hurried to tell you His answer. God has a plan for His people, the Jews. There are 490 years (*seventy sevens*) in His plan. (See **Daniel** 9:20-24.) During the first 49 years (*seven sevens*) the city of Jerusalem will be rebuilt. (And this came true!) After 434 more years (*sixty-two sevens*) Messiah, the Anointed One, will die (*will be cut off*)." (See **Daniel** 9:26. *Teacher:* 49 years + 434 years=483 years [of the 490 years in God's plan]. The last seven years are yet to come.)

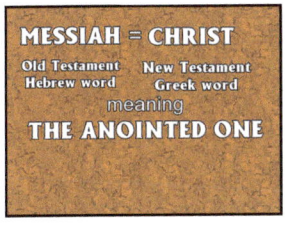

Show Back Cover

Did you hear what the angel said? MESSIAH, THE ANOINTED ONE! **Daniel** was the first to hear the name "Messiah." **Daniel** lived and died long, long before Messiah came. But in exactly the number of years that the angel Gabriel said, Christ the Messiah did die. His people, the Jews refused to trust in Him. They would not receive Him as their King. Indeed, they shouted, "Crucify Him!' We have no king but Caesar!" (See John 19:15.) So the remaining seven years in God's plan would have to wait.

Daniel (like the Prophets **Isaiah**, **Jeremiah** and **Ezekiel**) prophesied of Christ hundreds of years ahead of time.

(*Teacher:* To help students remember the names of the prophets and their prophecies, fill in names on dotted lines.)

Show Illustration #15A

Isaiah had prophesied (7:14) that a virgin would have a Son. (Print **ISAIAH** below manger.) The Son would be called "Immanuel" because of His being *God with us*. Immanuel, Christ, did come and was placed in a manger. (Print IMMANUEL above manger.)

Show Illustration #15B

Isaiah also prophesied of Christ's awful suffering (52:13-14; 53:3-7). And both Isaiah (53:8-9) and **Daniel** (9:26) foretold Christ's death. (On dotted lines print **ISAIAH** and **DANIEL**.)

Show Illustration #15C

JEREMIAH (33:14-17) prophesied that Christ would he a "Righteous Branch"–the One from David's family who would always do right. And **Isaiah** (9:7), **Jeremiah** (23:5-6), and **Ezekiel** (37:24-25) foretold that Christ would be the King. (Print prophets' names on dotted lines.) Christ will be King in the future Millennium. And, sitting on His throne in Jerusalem, Christ will then rule over all the earth.

Many, many prophecies have already been fulfilled. All the others will come true because God Himself spoke them to and through His prophets. God has plans for the Jews, the people He chose for Himself. And He will rule over them in His own way forever.

4. GOD'S RULE OVER EARTH
Daniel 12:1-13; Revelation 19:11-22:21

You remember that the angel Gabriel told **Daniel**, "God has a plan for His people. There are 490 years in His plan." Now listen very carefully! During the first 49 years of God's plan, Jerusalem city was rebuilt. After the next 434 years, Christ the Messiah died. Add 49 years to 434 years and that equals 483 years. That leaves seven years of the 490 years. Those seven years are yet to come some future day. (See **Daniel** 9:27.) Those seven years are called the *Tribulation*. They will be dreadful years of awful trouble. (See **Daniel** 12:1, 7; Matthew 24:4-28.) When that time comes, there will be no Christians on earth. For Christ Jesus will have already come in the air and caught them up to Heaven.

Show illustration #16A

There they will be with Him. (*Teacher:* Emphasize that Christ will come in the *air–not* to the *earth*. See 1 Corinthians 15:51-52; 1 Thessalonians 4:13-18).

All who have refused to receive Christ the Messiah will be left on earth. Here they will suffer dreadfully for seven awful years of tribulation.

Show Illustration #16B

The Tribulation will be much worse than anything we can imagine. There will be bloody wars, famines, earthquakes. Hail, fire, blood will cover the earth. The sun will become dark and the moon will turn red. Cities and seas will be destroyed. Thousands of people will die. And one who hates Christ (named the anti-Christ) will take over. (See **Daniel** 11:36-37; 1 John 2:18; Revelation 11:7; 13:7.)

After those seven terrifying years of Tribulation, Christ will return to earth. He will bring with Him all those who belong to Him. He will defeat Satan's army, chain Satan (in the abyss) for 1,000 years, and hurl anti-Christ into the lake of fire forever. (See Revelation 19:17-21.)

Show Illustration #16C

Then Christ the King will reign for 1,000 wonderful years of peace. (See Revelation 20:1-15.) Those peaceful years are called *The Millennium*. At the end of the Millennium, Satan and his followers will be set free for a short time.

Show Illustration #17A

With fire from heaven, God will then destroy Satan's people. And He will hurl Satan into the lake of fire forever. (See Revelation 20:7-10.) Any who have never believed in Christ will then be cast into the lake of fire. (See Revelation 20:15; 21:8.) And the heavens and the earth will be destroyed by fire. (See 2 Peter 3:10.)

Show Illustration #17B

Finally a new Holy City will come down from heaven. It will shine with the wonderful brightness of God's own glory. (See Revelation 21:10-11, 23.) God will sit on His throne and Christ with Him. And all who received Christ Jesus here on earth will be in that Holy City serving God the Father and Christ the Son. (See Revelation 22:3.) Will *you* be there? If you have any question in your mind, please talk to me about it after class.

MESSIANIC PROPHECIES

Taken from the RYRIE STUDY BIBLE (N.I.V.) By Charles Caldwell Ryrie, Th.D., Ph.D. Copyright 1986. Moody Bible Institute of Chicago. Moody Press. Used by Permission.

Topic	Old Testament Prophecy	New Testament Fulfillment
Messiah to be the seed of the woman	Genesis 3:15	Galatians 4:4
Messiah to be the seed of Abraham	Genesis 12:3; 18:18	Luke 3:34 Matthew 1:2 Acts 3:25 Galatians 3:16
Messiah to be of the tribe of Judah	Genesis 49:10	Luke 3:33 Matthew 1:2
Messiah to be of the seed of Jacob	Numbers 24:17, 19	Matthew 1:2 Luke 3:34
Messiah to be of the seed of David	Psalm 132:11 Jeremiah 23:5; 33:15 Isaiah 11:10	Matthew 1:6 Luke 1:32-33 Romans 1:3 Acts 2:30
Messiah to be a prophet like Moses	Deuteronomy 18:15, 19	Matthew 21:11 John 1:45 John 6:14 Acts 3:22-23
Messiah to be the Son of God	Psalm 2:7 (Proverbs 30:4)	Luke 1:32 Matthew 3:17
Messiah to be raised from the dead	Psalm 16:10	Acts 13:35-37
The crucifixion experience	Psalm 22 Psalm 69:21	Matthew 27:34-50 John 19:28-30
Messiah to be betrayed by a friend	Psalm 41:9	John 13:18, 21
Messiah ascends to heaven	Psalm 68:18	Luke 24:51 Acts 1:9
Homage and tribute paid to Messiah by great kings	Psalm 72:10-11	Matthew 2:1-11
Messiah to be a priest like Melchizedek	Psalm 110:4	Hebrews 5:5-6
Messiah to be at the right hand of God	Psalm 110:1	Matthew 27:64 Hebrews 1:3
Messiah, the stone the builders rejected, to become the head cornerstone	Psalm 118:22-23 Isaiah 8:14-15 Isaiah 28:16	Matthew 21:42-43 Acts 4:11 Romans 1:32-33 Ephesians 2:20 1 Peter 2:6-8
Messiah to be born of a virgin	Isaiah 7:14	Matthew 1:18-25 Luke 1:26-35
Galilee to be the first area of Messiah's ministry	Isaiah 9:1-8	Matthew 4:12-16
Messiah will be meek and mild	Isaiah 42:2-3 Isaiah 53:7	Matthew 12:18-20 Matthew 26:62-63
Messiah will minister to the Gentiles	Isaiah 42:1 Isaiah 49:1-8	Matthew 12:21
Messiah will be smitten	Isaiah 50:6	Matthew 26:67 Matthew 27:26, 30
The gospel according to Isaiah (The suffering Messiah brings salvation)	Isaiah 52:13-53:12	The four gospels
The New and Everlasting Covenant	Isaiah 55:3-4 Jeremiah 31:31-33	Matthew 26:28 Mark 14:24 Luke 22:20 Hebrews 8:6-13
Messiah, the Right Arm of God	Isaiah 59:16 Isaiah 53:1	John 12:38
Messiah as Intercessor	Isaiah 59:16	Hebrews 9:15
Twofold mission of the Messiah	Isaiah 61:1-11	Luke 4:16-21
Messiah will perform miracles	Isaiah 35:5-6	John 11:47 Matthew 11:3-6
Messiah is called "The Lord"	Jeremiah 23:5-6	Acts 2:36
The time of Messiah's coming prophesied	Daniel 9:24-26	Galatians 4:4 Ephesians 1:10
Bethlehem to be the place of Messiah's birth	Micah 5:2	Matthew 2:1 Luke 2:4-6
Messiah will enter the Temple with authority	Malachi 3:1	Matthew 21:12
Messiah will enter Jerusalem on a donkey	Zechariah 9:9	Matthew 21:1-10
Messiah will be pierced	Zechariah 12:10 Psalm 22:16	John 19:34, 37
Messiah to be forsaken by His disciples	Zechariah 13:7	Matthew 26:32, 56
The coming of the Holy Spirit in the days of the Messiah	Joel 2:28	Acts 2:16-18
Opposition of the nations	Psalm 2:2	Revelation 19:19
Messiah's final victory over death	Isaiah 25:8	1 Corinthians 15:54 Revelation 7:17; 21:4
The glorious Messiah	Isaiah 63:1	Revelation 19:11-16
Messiah as King	Psalm 2:6-9	Revelation 19:15-16
Submission of all nations to Messiah's rule	Isaiah 2:4 Micah 4:1-4	Revelation 12:5
The Gentiles shall seek the Messiah of Israel	Isaiah 11:10	Romans 11:25

NOTE TO THE TEACHER

For the most part, this VISUALIZED BIBLE series follows the Biblical order of the books. However, Old Testament Volumes 24, 25, and 26 are taught chronologically. Examine the excellent charts below. Immediately you will understand the importance of including the nine Minor Prophets in these volumes.

The arrangement of the books of the Old Testament does not follow the chronological order in which the recorded events occurred. The following listing shows which books cover approximately the same periods of time.

- Genesis and Job
- Exodus and Leviticus
- Numbers and Deuteronomy
- Joshua
- Judges and Ruth
- 1 Samuel
- 2 Samuel and Psalms
- 1 King with 1 Chronicles, Song of Solomon, Proverbs, and Ecclesiastes
- 2 Kings with 2 Chronicles, Obadiah, Joel, Jonah, Amos, Hosea, Micah, Isaiah, Nahum, Zephaniah, Habakkuk, Jeremiah, and Lamentations
- Daniel and Ezekiel
- Ezra with Esther, Haggai, and Zechariah
- Nehemiah and Malachi

THE PROPHETIC BOOKS

Taken from RYRIE STUDY BIBLE (NIV) (Moody Press material). Copyright 1977, 1978 on the RSB version by Moody Bible Institute of Chicago. Moody Press. *Charts used by permission.*

	Book	Date	Background Scripture	Kings (N=north; S=south)	
Before the Exile	Obadiah	840	2 Kings 8:12	Jehoram, Ahaziah, Athaliah, Joash (S)	Judgment on Edom
	Joel	835	2 Kings 12	Joash (S)	Plague of locusts
	Jonah	760	2 Kings 14	Jeroboam II (N)	Nineveh, repent!
	Amos	755	2 Kings 14	Jeroboam II (N)	Social evils
	Hosea	710	2 Kings 14-17	Jeroboam II, Zechariah, Shallum, Menahem, Pekiah, Pekah, Hoshea (N)	God's steadfast love
	Isaiah	740-680	2 Kings 15-21	Jotham, Ahaz, Hezekiah, Manasseh (S)	Messiah's salvation
	Micah	700	2 Kings 15-20	Jotham, Ahaz, Hezekiah (S)	Doom and deliverance
	Nahum	663-612	2 Kings 21-23	Manasseh, Amon, Josiah (S)	Destruction of Nineveh
	Zephaniah	625	2 Kings 22-23	Josiah (S)	Judgment on Judah
	Habakkuk	607	2 Kings 22-24	Josiah, Jehoahaz, Jehoiakim (S)	Babylonian captivity
	Jeremiah	627-585		Josiah, Jehoahaz, Jehoiakim, Jehoiachin, Zedekiah (S), Nebuchadnezzar of Babylon	Judgment for backsliding
During the Exile	Lamentations	586-585	2 Kings 25	Nebuchadnezzar	Mourning over the destruction of Jerusalem and the Temple
	Ezekiel	592-570	2 Kings 24-25	Zedekiah (S)	God keeps His covenant
	Daniel	537	2 Kings 23-25; Ezra 1-4	Jehoiakim (S), Nebuchadnezzar, Belshazzar, Darius, Cyrus	God's plan for the future
After the Exile	Haggai	520	Ezra 5-6	Zerubbabel, Darius I	Rebuild the Temple
	Zechariah	520-518	Ezra 5-6	Zerubbabel, Darius I, Xerxes	Hope in the return of Christ
	Malachi	450-400	Nehemiah 13	Artaxerxes, Darius II	God's complaint against Israel

MAPS OF EMPIRES

MAPS OF EMPIRES

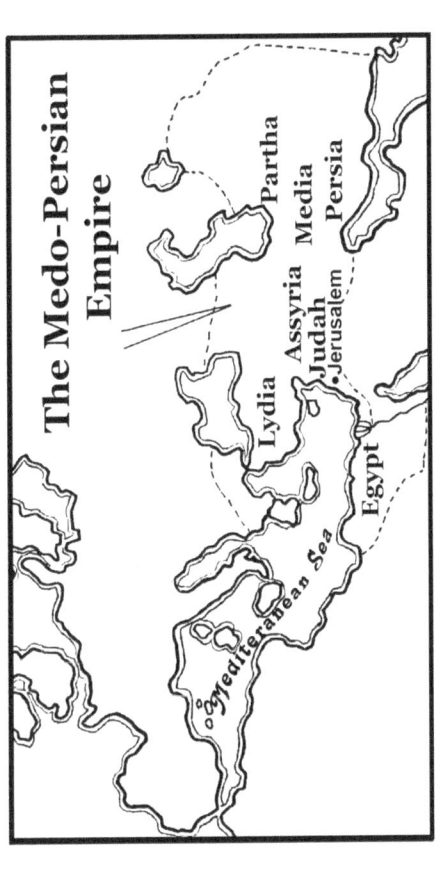

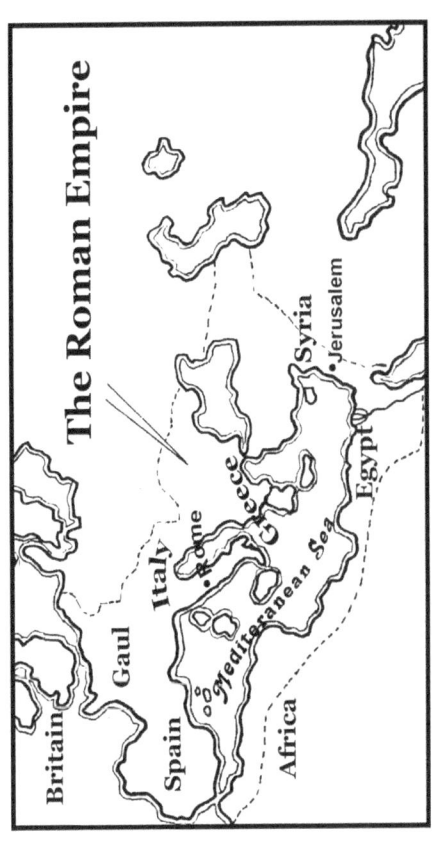

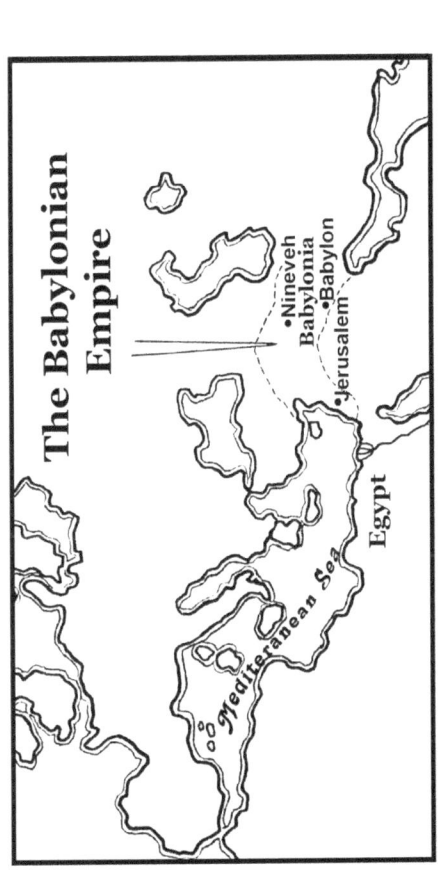

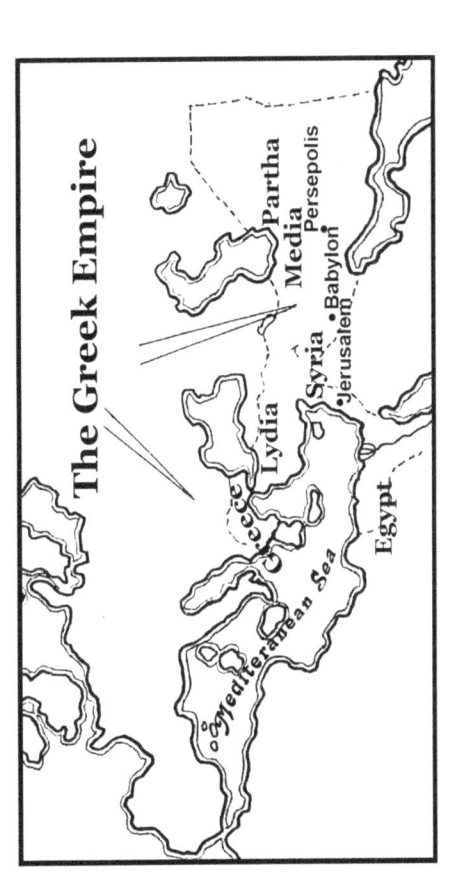

© Bible Visuals International Inc

www.ingramcontent.com/pod-product-compliance
Lightning Source LLC
Chambersburg PA
CBHW060759090426
42736CB00002B/87